A Primer of Forestry

CONTENTS.

3

ILLUSTRATIONS.

4

A PRIMER OF FORESTRY.

THE LIFE OF A TREE.

The object of forestry is to discover and apply the principles according to which forests are best managed. It is distinct from arboriculture, which deals with individual trees. Forestry has to do with single trees only as they stand together on some large area whose principal crop is trees, and which therefore forms part of a forest. The forest is the most highly organized portion of the vegetable world. It takes its importance less from the individual trees which help to form it than from the qualities which belong to it as a whole. Although it is composed of trees, the forest is far more than a collection of trees standing in one place. It has a population of animals and plants peculiar to itself, a soil largely of its own making, and a climate different in many ways from that of the open country. Its influence upon the streams alone makes farming possible in many regions, and everywhere it tends to prevent floods and drought. It supplies fuel, one of the first necessaries of life, and lumber, the raw material, without which cities, railroads, and all the great achievements of material progress would have been either long delayed or wholly impossible. The forest is as beautiful as it is useful. The old fairy tales which spoke of it as a terrible place are wrong. No one can really know the forest without feeling the gentle influence of one of the kindliest and

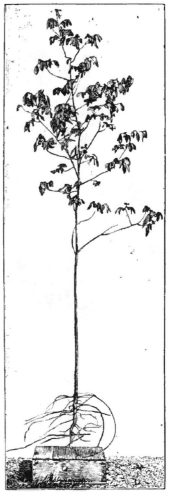

Fig. 1.—Roots, stem, and crown of a young Shellbark Hickory.

strongest parts of nature. From every point of view it is one of the most helpful friends of man. Perhaps no other natural agent has done so much for the human race and has been so recklessly used and so little understood.

THE PARTS OF A TREE.

In order rightly to understand the forest, something must first be known about the units of which it is made up. A tree, then, is a woody plant growing up from the ground usually with a single stem (fig. 1). It consists of three parts: (1) The roots (fig. 2), which extend into the

FIG. 2.—Upturned skeleton roots of a Red Fir. The small roots have been burned away and the others cleared of soil by the fire. Olympic Peninsula, Washington.

ground to a depth of 3 or 4 feet, or still farther when the soil is not too hard and they do not find moisture enough near the surface; they hold the tree in place and take up from the soil water and certain mineral substances which the tree needs in its growth; (2) the trunk or stem (fig. 3), which supports the crown and supplies it with mineral food and water from the roots; (3) the crown itself (fig. 4), with its network of branches, buds, and leaves, in which the food taken up by the tree from the soil and air is worked over and made ready to assist in the growth of the whole plant.

The crown has more to do with the life of the tree than its other parts, for the most important processes in the reproduction of the tree nd the digestion of its food take place in the crown. For this reason, nd because we can control its shape and size more easily and directly han that of the roots or trunk, the crown is of special interest to the orester. It is almost exclusively with the crowns that he has to deal n tending a crop of trees and preparing the way for the succeeding

Fig. 3.—Trunks of two Red Firs of great size, Olympic Forest Reserve, Washington.

Fig. 4.—Stem and crown of a Longleaf Pine, the latter covered with moss swaying in the wind.

generation. As they stand together in the forest, the crowns of the rees form a broken shelter, which is usually spoken of as the leaf anopy, but which may better be called the cover.

THE FOOD OF A TREE.

The materials upon which a tree feeds are derived from the soil and he air. The minute root hairs which spring from the rootlets take ap water from the ground, and with it various substances which it holds in solution. These are the earthy constituents of the tree, which reappear in the form of ashes when any part of it is burned. The water which contains these materials goes straight from the roots to the leaves, in which a most important process in the feeding of the tree takes place. The process is the assimilation or taking up and breaking up, by the leaves, of carbonic-acid gas from the air. It goes on only in the presence of light and heat, and through the action of chlorophyll, a substance from which the leaves and the young bark get their green color.

Plants containing chlorophyll are the chief means by which mineral materials are changed into food, so that nearly all plant and animal life depends upon them. Plant cells which contain chlorophyll break up the carbonic-acid gas with which they come in contact, retain the carbon, one of its elements, and send back the other, oxygen, into the air. Then, still under the influence of the sunlight, they combine the carbon with the oxygen and hydrogen of the water from the roots into new chemical compounds, in which nitrogen and the earthy constituents mentioned above are also present; that is to say, the food materials which reach the tree through the roots and leaves are first digested in the leaves somewhat as food is digested in the human body, and are then sent to all living parts of the roots, stem, and crown, where they pass through another process of digestion, and are then either used at once in growth or stored away until the proper moment arrives. This is the general rule, but it is believed that in some cases food taken up by the roots can be used without first being digested in the leaves.

THE COMPOSITION OF WOOD.

Wood is made up chiefly of carbon, oxygen, and hydrogen. When perfectly dry, about half its weight is carbon, and half oxygen and hydrogen, in almost the same proportion as in water. It contains also about 1 part in 100, by weight, of earthy constituents, and nitrogen to the same amount. When wood is burned, all these materials disappear into the air except the earthy constituents. Now, the nitrogen and water taken up by the roots were originally in the air before they reached the ground. It is true, therefore, that when wood is burned those parts of it which came from the air go back into it in the form of gas, while those which came from the soil remain behind in the form of ashes.

HOW THE TREE BREATHES.

Besides giving out oxygen in assimilation, trees also take in oxygen from the air through their leaves, and through the minute openings in the bark called lenticels, such as the oblong raised spots or marks

173

on the young branches of birch and cherry and many other trees. All plants, like all animals, breathe; and plants, like animals, breathe in oxygen and breathe out carbonic acid gas. This process of respiration or the breathing of the tree goes on both day and night, but it is far less active than assimilation, which takes place only in the light. Consequently more carbonic-acid gas is taken into the tree than is given out, and the surplus carbon remains to be used in growing.

TRANSPIRATION.

The leaves give out not only the oxygen derived from the decomposition of carbonic-acid gas taken from the air and carbonic-acid gas produced in breathing, but also great quantities of water vapor. The amount of water taken up by the roots is very much larger than is required to be combined with carbon and the earthy constituents in the leaves. In order that fresh supplies of earthy constituents in solution may reach the leaves rapidly the water already in them must be got out of the way. This is effected by transpiration, which is the evaporation of water from all parts of the tree above ground, but principally from the leaves. Even where the bark is very thick, as on the trunks of old oaks and chestnuts, transpiration goes on through the lenticels in the bottoms of the deep cracks (fig. 5).

FIG. 5.—Cross section of wood and bark of the Western Yellow Pine, showing two of the deep cracks in the bark, at the bottom of which lenticels are placed.

It sometimes happens, especially in spring before the leaves come out, that transpiration can not get rid of the water from the roots as fast as it rises, and that it falls in drops from the buds, or later on even from the leaves themselves.

THE GROWTH OF A TREE.

The addition of new material in the way described in the preceding pages is the foundation of growth. Except in the buds, leaves, fruit, and the twigs less than a year old, this material is deposited in a thin coat over the whole tree between the wood and the bark. The new twigs grow in length by a kind of stretching, but only during the first year. Thus it is only by means of these youngest twigs that a

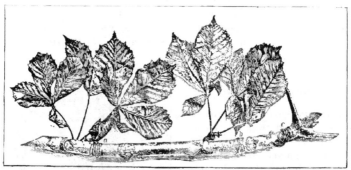

Fig. 6.—Yearly growth of a branch of Horse Chestnut. The bands of wrinkles mark the divisions between the growths of four successive years. The distance between these bands would never have been greater than it was when the branch was cut.

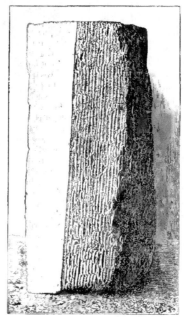

Fig. 7.—Perpendicular cut of wood and bark of the Western Yellow Pine, showing the division of the bark into scales by the successive layers of cork cambium. The true cambium is between wood and bark.

tree increases in height and in spread of branches. After the first year their length is fixed, younger twigs stretch out from the buds,

nd the older ones grow henceforth only in thickness (fig. 6). The
resh coat of new material mentioned above covers them year by year.
'here are two layers in this coat, separated by a third one of tender
orming tissues called the cambium, in which the actual making of the
ew substance goes on. The inner side of the cambium layer forms
ew wood, the outer side new bark. Besides the true cambium, which
orms both wood and bark, there is another cambium which makes
ae corky outer bark and nothing else (figs. 7 and 8). This cork
ambium may encircle the whole tree, like the true cambium, as in the

FIG. 8.—Outer surface of bark of the Western Yellow Pine, showing the scales made by the successive
layers of cork cambium.

led Cedar, or it may form little separate films in the bark, but in
ither case it dies from time to time, and is re-formed nearer the wood.

THE STRUCTURE OF WOOD.

Wood is chiefly made up of very small tubes or cells (fig. 9) of vari-
us kinds, which have special uses in the life of the tree. Some con-
net water from the roots to the crown, some store away digested
ood, and others merely strengthen the structure of the wood and hold
together. The wood of cone-bearing or coniferous trees (like the
ines and spruces) has but few kinds of cells, while that of the broad-
af trees (such as oaks and maples) is much less simple. But in each
ase some of the cells have thick walls and small openings, and others
ide openings and very thin walls. In climates which have regularly
ne season of growth and one of rest, like our own, the cells of the

173

layer of new wood formed each year at the inner surface of the cambium are arranged in a definite way. When growth begins in the spring, and the fresh twigs and leaves put out, there is a great demand for water in the crown to supply these moist green new parts of the tree. Water rises in most trees through the newer layers of the wood, and especially through the last ring. Consequently, at first the tree makes thin-walled cells with wide openings, through which water can rise rapidly to the ends of the branches. Later on, when the demand for water is not so great, and there is plenty of digested food to supply building material, the cells formed are narrow and thick-walled. Thus the summer wood in each year's growth is heavier, stronger, and darker in color than the spring wood. In the wood of many broadleaf trees, such as oak and chestnut, the spring wood is also marked by a band of open tubes of larger size called ducts. In others, such as maple and beech, these ducts are scattered through the whole season's growth, and in all conifers, as for example the pines and cedars, they are entirely wanting. But the differences in hardness and color between the growth of spring and summer are still present. It is sometimes possible to see the line which separates the growth of two seasons in the bark, as in the case of common cork, which is the outer bark of the Cork Oak, a native of southern Europe.

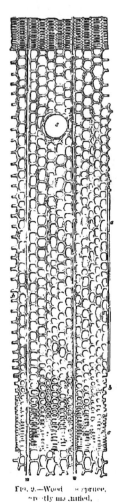

Fig. 9.—Wood of spruce, greatly magnified.

If the trunk or branch of an oak tree is cut smoothly across, thin whitish lines may be seen running from within outward (fig. 10, block at the right). Some of these lines begin in the center of the tree and others in each one of the annual rings. These are the medullary rays, which make the silver grain in quartered oak and other woods. They exist in all kinds of trees, but in many as, for example, in the Chestnut and in most conifers they are so fine as hardly to be seen with the naked eye. Seasoning cracks which run across the rings of growth always follow the lines of these rays, while others most often follow along some annual ring.

ANNUAL RINGS.

It is correct to speak of these rings of growth as "annual rings," or as long as the tree is growing healthily a ring is formed each year

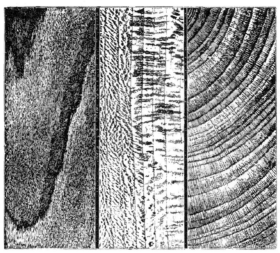

FIG. 10.—Wood of Western Hemlock.

igs. 10, 11). It is true that two false rings may appear in one year, ut they are generally so much thinner than the rings on each side that is not hard to detect them. Very ften they do not extend entirely round the tree, as a true ring always oes if the tree is sound. Whenever ie growth of the tree is interrupted nd begins again during the same eason, such a false ring is formed. his happens when the foliage is estroyed by caterpillars and grows gain in the same season, or when very severe drought in early sum-

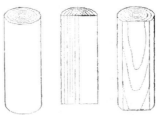

FIG. 11.—Annual rings.

ier stops growth for a time, after late frosts, and in similar cases.

HEARTWOOD AND SAPWOOD.

An annual layer once formed does not change in size or place during ie healthy life of the tree, except that it is covered in time by other, ounger layers. A nail driven into a tree 6 feet from the ground will ill be at the same height after it is buried under 20 or 50 or 100 yers of annual growth. But in most trees, like the oaks and pines, ie wood becomes darker in color and harder after it has been in the tree for some years. The openings of its cells become choked so that the sap can no longer run through them. From living sapwood, in which growth is going on, it becomes heartwood, which is dead, because it has nothing to do with growth (fig. 12). It is simply a strong framework which helps to support the living parts of the tree. This is why hollow trees may flourish and bear fruit. When the tree is cut down, the sapwood rots more easily than the heartwood, because

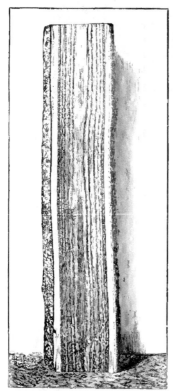

it takes up water readily and contains plant food, which decays very fast. Not all trees have heartwood, and in many the difference in color between it and the sapwood is very slight. Since water from the roots rises only in the sapwood, it is easy to kill trees with heartwood by girdling them, provided all the sapwood is cut through. But in those which have no heartwood the tubes of the older layers of wood can still convey water to the crown, and when such trees are girdled it is often several years before they die.

A great many theories have been proposed to account for the rise of water into the tops of tall trees, some of which, as in the big trees of California, may be over 300 feet from the ground. But none of these theories is quite satisfactory, and it must be admitted that we do not yet know how the trees supply their lofty crowns with the water which keeps them alive.

FIG. 12.—A section of the common Staghorn Sumach, showing the darkened heartwood, the white sapwood, and the inner and outer bark. Milford, Pa.

TREES IN THE FOREST.

The nature of a tree, as shown by its behavior in the forest, is called its silvicultural character. It is made up of all those qualities upon which the species as a whole, and every individual tree, depend in their struggle for existence. The regions in which a tree will live, and the places where it will flourish best; the trees it will grow with, and those which it kills or is killed by; its abundance or scarcity; its size and rate of growth all these things are decided by the inborn qualities, or silvicultural character, of each particular kind of tree.

THE VARIOUS REQUIREMENTS OF TREES.

Different species of trees, like different races of men, have special requirements for the things upon which their life depends. Some races, like the Eskimos, live only in cold regions. Others, like the South Sea Islanders, must have a very warm climate to be comfortable, and are short-lived in any other (fig. 13). So it is with trees, except that their different needs are even more varied and distinct. Some of them, like the willows, birches, and spruces of northern Canada, stand on the boundary of tree growth within the Arctic Circle. Other species grow only in tropical lands, and can not resist even the

Fig. 13.—A forest of palms in southern Florida.

ightest frost. It is always the highest and lowest temperature, rather han the average, which decides where a tree will or will not grow. Thus the average temperature of an island where it never freezes may e only 60°, while another place, with an average of 70°, may have occasional frosts. Trees which could not live at all in the latter on account of the frost might flourish in the lower average warmth of he former.

In this way the influence of heat and cold on trees has a great leal to do with their distribution over the surface of the whole earth. Their distribution within shorter distances also often depends largely upon it. In the United States, for example, the Live Oak does not grow in Maine nor the Canoe Birch in Florida. Even the opposite sides of the same hill may be covered with two different species, because one of them resists the late and early frosts and the fierce midday heat of summer, while the other requires the coolness and moisture of the northern slope (fig. 14). On the eastern slopes, where the sun strikes early in the day, frosts in the spring and fall are far more apt to kill the young trees or the blossoms and twigs of older

FIG. 14. The Black Hemlock in its home, Cascade Mountains of Washington.

ones than on those which face to the west and north, where growth begins later in the spring, and where rapid thawing, which does more harm than the freezing itself, is less likely to take place.

REQUIREMENTS OF TREES FOR HEAT AND MOISTURE.

Heat and moisture act together upon trees in such a way that it is sometimes hard to distinguish their effects. A dry country or a dry slope is apt to be hot as well, while a cool northern slope is almost always moister than one turned toward the south. Still the results of he demand of trees for water can usually be distinguished from the results of their need of warmth, and it is found that moisture has almost as great an influence on the distribution of trees over the earth is heat itself. Indeed, within any given region it is apt to be much more conspicuous, and the smaller the region the more noticeable often s its effect, because the contrast is more striking. Thus it is frequently easy to see the difference between the trees in a swamp and hose on a dry hillside nearby, when it would be far less easy to distinguish the general character of the forest which includes both swamp and hillside from that of another forest at a distance. In many nstances the demand for water controls distribution altogether. For his reason the forests on the opposite sides of mountain ranges are often composed of entirely different trees. On the west slope of the Sierra Nevada of California, for example, where there is plenty of noisture, there is also one of the most beautiful of all forests. The east slope, on the contrary, has comparatively few trees, because its rainfall s very slight, and those which do grow there are small and stunted in comparison with the giants on the west. Again, certain trees, like the Bald Cypress and the River Birch, are commonly found only in very moist land; others, like the mesquites and the Pinyon or Nut Pine, only on the driest soils; while still others, like the Red Cedar and the Red Fir, seem to adapt themselves to almost any degree of moisture, and are found on both very wet and very dry soils. In this way the different demands for moisture often separate the kinds of trees which grow in the bottom of a valley from those along its slopes, or even hose in the gullies of hillsides from those on the rolling land between. A mound not more than a foot above the level of a swamp is often covered with trees entirely different from those of the wetter lower and about it.

Such matters as these have far more to do with the places in which different trees grow than the chemical composition of the soil. But its mechanical nature—that is, whether it is stiff or loose, fine or coarse in grain, deep or shallow—is very important, because it is directly connected with heat and moisture and the life of the roots in the soil.

REQUIREMENTS OF TREES FOR LIGHT.

The relations of trees to heat and moisture are thus largely responsible for their distribution upon the great divisions of the earth's surface, such as continents and mountain ranges, as well as over the smaller rises and depressions of every region where trees grow. But while heat and moisture decide where the different kinds of trees can grow, their influence has comparatively little to do with the struggles of individuals or species against each other for the actual possession of the ground. The outcome of these struggles depends less on heat and moisture than on the possession of certain qualities, among which is the ability to bear shade. With regard to this power trees are roughly divided into two classes, often called shade-bearing and light-demanding, following the German, but better named tolerant and intolerant of shade. Tolerant trees are those which flourish under more or less heavy shade in early youth; intolerant trees are those which demand a comparatively slight cover, or even unrestricted light. Later in life all trees require much more light than at first, and usually those of both classes can live to old age only when they are altogether unshaded from above. But there is always this difference between them: The leaves of tolerant trees will bear more shade. Consequently the leaves on the lower and inner parts of the crown are more vigorous, plentiful, and persistent than is the case with intolerant trees. Thus the crown of a tolerant tree in the forest is usually denser and longer than that of one which bears less shade. It is usually true that the seedlings of trees with dense crowns are able to flourish under cover, while those of light-crowned trees are intolerant. This rough general rule is often of use in the study of forests in a new country, or of trees whose silvicultural character is not known.

TOLERANCE AND INTOLERANCE.

The tolerance or intolerance of trees is one of their most important silvicultural characters. Frequently it is the first thing a forester seeks to learn about them, because what he can safely undertake in the woods depends so largely upon it. Thus tolerant trees will often grow vigorously under the shade of light-crowned trees (fig. 15) above them, while if the positions were reversed the latter would speedily die. The proportion of different kinds of trees in a forest often depends on their tolerance. Thus hemlock sometimes replaces White Pine in Pennsylvania, because it can grow beneath the pine, and so be ready to fill the opening whenever a pine dies. But the pine can not grow under the hemlock, and can only take possession of the ground when a fire or a windfall makes an opening where it can have plenty of light. Some trees after being overshaded can never recover their vigor when at last they are set free. Others do recover and grow vigorously even after many years of starving under heavy shade. The Red Spruce in the Adirondacks has a wonderful power of this kind, and makes a fine tree after spending the first fifty or even one hundred years of its life in reaching a diameter of two inches.

The relation of a tree to light changes not only with its age, but also with the place where it is growing, and with its health. An intolerant tree will stand more cover where the light is intense than in a cloudy northern region, and more if it has plenty of water than

vith a scanty supply. Vigorous seedlings will get along with less
ight than sickly ones. Seedlings of the same species will prosper
under heavier shade if they have always grown under cover than if
hey have had plenty of light at first and have been deprived of it
fterwards.

Fig. 15.—Young oaks starting under an old forest of pines. Eastern North Carolina.

THE RATE OF GROWTH.

The rate of growth of different trees often decides which one will
urvive in the forest. For example, if two intolerant kinds of trees
hould start together on a burned area or an old field, that one which
grows faster in height will overtop the other and destroy it in the
nd by cutting off the light. Some trees, like the Black Walnut, grow
apidly from their earliest youth. Others grow very slowly for the
irst few years. The stem of the Longleaf Pine, at 4 years old, is
usually not more than 5 inches in length. During this time the roots
ave been growing instead of the stem. The period of its rapid
growth in height comes later.

The place where a tree stands has a great influence on its rate of
growth. Thus the trees on a hillside are often much smaller than
hose of equal age in the rich hollow below, and those on the upper

slopes of a high mountain are commonly starved and stunted in comparison with the vigorous forest lower down. The Western Chinquapin, which reaches a height of 150 feet in the coast valleys of northern California, is a mere shrub at high elevations in the Sierra Nevada. The same thing is often observed in passing from the more temperate regions to the far north. Thus the Canoe Birch, at its northern limit, rises only a few inches above the ground, while farther south it becomes a tree sometimes 120 feet in height.

THE REPRODUCTIVE POWER OF TREES.

Another matter which is of the deepest interest to the forester is the reproductive power of his trees. Except in the case of sprouts and other growth fed by old roots, this depends first of all on the quantity of the seed which each tree bears; but so many other considerations affect the result that a tree which bears seed abundantly may not reproduce itself very well. A part of the seed is always unsound, and sometimes much the larger part, as in the case of the Tulip Tree. But even a great abundance of sound seed does not always insure good reproduction. The seeds may not find the right

FIG. 16 Winged seeds 1, Basswood, 2 Boxelder 3, Elm, 4 3 Pine.

surroundings for successful germination, or the infant trees may perish for want of water, light, or suitable soil. Where there is a thick layer of dry leaves or needles on the ground, seedlings often perish in great numbers because their delicate rootlets can not reach the fertile soil beneath. The same thing happens when there is no humus at all and the surface is hard and dry. The weight of the seed also has a powerful influence on the character of reproduction. Trees with heavy seeds, like oaks, hickories, and chestnuts, can sow them only in their own neighborhood, except when they stand on steep hillsides or on the banks of streams, or when birds and squirrels carry the nuts and acorns to a distance. Trees with light, winged seeds (fig. 16), like the poplars, birches, and pines, have a great advantage over the others, because they can drop their seeds a long way off. The wind is the means by which this is brought about, and the adaptation of the seeds themselves is often very curious and interesting. The wing of a pine seed, for example, is so placed that the seed whirls when it falls, in such a way that it falls very slowly. Thus the wind has time to carry it away before it can reach the ground. In heavy winds pine and other winged seeds are blown long distances—sometimes as much as several miles. This explains how certain kinds of trees, like the Gray Birch and the White Pine, grow up in the middle of open pastures, and how others, such as the Lodgepole Pine, cover great areas, far from the parent trees, with young growth of even age.

Such facts help to explain why, in certain places, it happens that when pines are cut down oaks succeed them, or when oaks are removed pines occupy the ground. It is very often true that young trees of one kind are already growing unnoticed beneath old trees of another, and so are ready to replace them whenever the old trees are cut away.

PURE AND MIXED FOREST.

The nature of the seed has much to do with the distribution of trees in pure or mixed forest. Some kinds of trees usually grow in bodies of some extent containing only a single kind; in other words, in pure forest. The Longleaf Pine of the South Atlantic and Gulf States is of this kind, and so is the Lodgepole Pine of the West. Conifers are more apt to grow in pure forest than broadleaf trees, because it is more common for them to have winged seeds. The greater part of the heavy-seeded trees in the United States are deciduous, and most of the deciduous trees grow in mixed forest, although there are some conspicuous exceptions. But even in mixed forests small groups of trees with heavy seeds are common, because the young trees naturally start up beneath and around the old ones. A heavy seed, dropping from the top of a tall tree, often strikes the lower branches in its fall and bounds far outside the circle of the crown. Trees which are found only, or most often, in pure forest are the social or gregarious kinds; those which grow in mixture with other trees are called scattered kinds. Most of the hardwood forests in the United States are mixed; and many mixed forests, like that in the Adirondacks, contain both broadleaf trees and conifers. The line between gregarious and scattered species is not always well marked, because it often happens that a tree may be gregarious in one place and live with many others elsewhere. The Western Yellow Pine, which forms, on the plateau of central Arizona, perhaps the largest pure pine forest of the earth, is frequently found growing with other species in the mountains, especially in the Sierra Nevada of central California.

Trees which occupy the ground to the exclusion of all others do so because they succeed better, under the conditions, than their competi-

Fig. 17.—Chestnut sprouts from the stump.

tors. It may be that they are able to get on with less water, or to grow on poorer soil, their rate of growth or power of reproduction may be greater, or there may be some other reason why they are better fitted for their surroundings. But the gregarious trees are not all alike in their ability to sustain themselves in different situations, while the differences between some of the mixed-forest species are very marked indeed. Thus, Black Walnut, as a rule, grows only in rich, moist soil and Beech only in damp situations. Fire Cherry, on the other hand, is most common on lands which have been devastated by fire, and the Rock Oak is most often found on dry, barren ridges. The Tupelo or Black Gum and the Red Maple both grow best in swamps, but it is a common thing to find them also on dry, stony soils at a distance from water. The knowledge of such qualities as these is of great importance in the management of forest lands.

REPRODUCTION BY SPROUTS.

Besides reproduction from seed, which plays so large a part in the struggle for the ground, reproduction by sprouts from old roots or stumps (fig. 17) is of great importance in forestry. Trees differ very much in their power of sprouting. In nearly all conifers except the California coast Redwood, which has this ability beyond almost every other tree, it is lacking altogether. The Pitch or Jack Pine of the Eastern United States has it also to some extent, but in most places the sprouts usually die in early youth and seldom make merchantable trees. In the broadleaf kinds, on the other hand, it is a general and very valuable quality. Young stumps, as a rule, are much more productive than old ones, although some prolific species, like the Chestnut, sprout plentifully in old age. Other species, like the Beech, furnish numerous sprouts from young stumps and very few or none at all from old ones, and still others never sprout freely even in early youth.

THE LIFE OF A FOREST.

The history of the life of a forest is a story of the help and harm which the trees receive from one another. On one side every tree is engaged in a relentless struggle against its neighbors for light, water, and food, the three things trees need most. On the other side, each tree is constantly working with all its neighbors, even those which stand at some distance, to bring about the best condition of the soil and air for the growth and fighting power of every other tree.

A COMMUNITY OF TREES.

The life of a community of trees is an exceedingly interesting one. A forest tree is in many ways as much dependent upon its neighbors for safety and food as are the inhabitants of a town upon one another. The difference is that in a town each citizen has a special calling or occupation in which he works for the service of the commonwealth, while in the forest every tree contributes to the general welfare in nearly all the ways in which it is benefited by the community. A forest tree helps to protect its neighbors against the wind, which might overthrow them, and the sun, which is ready to dry up the soil about their roots or to make sun cracks in their bark by shining too hotly upon it (fig. 18). It enriches the earth in which they stand by the fall of its leaves and twigs, and aids in keeping the air about their crowns, and the soil about their roots, cooler in summer and warmer in winter than it would be if each tree stood alone. With the others it forms a

FIG. 18.—Forest trees standing too far apart to help each other. Lake Chelan, Washington.

common canopy under which the seedlings of all the members of this protective union are sheltered in early youth, and through which the beneficent influence of the forest is preserved and extended far beyond the spread of the trees themselves. But while this fruitful cooperation exists, there is also present, just as in a village or a city, a vigorous strife for the good things of life. For a tree the best of these, and often the hardest to get, are water for the roots and space and light for the crown. In all but very dry places there is water enough for

173

all the trees, and often more than enough, as for example in the Adirondack forest. The struggle for space and light is thus more important than the struggle for water, and as it takes place above ground it is also much more easily observed and studied.

Light and space are of such importance because, as we have seen, the leaves can not assimilate or digest food except in the presence of light and air. The rate at which a tree can grow and make new wood is decided chiefly by its ability to assimilate and digest plant food. This power depends upon the number, size, and health of the leaves, and these in turn upon the amount of space and light which the tree can secure.

THE LIFE OF A FOREST CROP.

The story of the life of a forest crop is then largely an account of the competition of the trees for light and room, and, although the very strength which enables them to carry on the fight is a result of their association, still the deadly struggle, in which the victims are many times more in number than those which survive, is apt alone to absorb the attention. Yet the mutual help of the trees to each other is always going quietly on. Every tree continually comforts and assists the other trees, which are its friendly enemies.

The purpose here is to follow the progress of a forest crop of uniform age from the seed through all the successive phases of its life until it reaches maturity, bears seed in its turn, and finally declines in fertility and

Fig. 19.—A White Pine seedling, showing the slender roots.

strength until at last it passes away and its place is filled by a new generation. The life history which we are about to follow, as it unfolds itself through the course of several hundred years, is full of struggle and danger in youth, restful and dignified in age. The changes which pass over it are vast and full of the deepest interest, but they are very gradual. From beginning to end one stage melts insensibly into the next. Still, in order to study and describe them conveniently, each stage must have limits and a name.

THE SEVEN AGES OF A TREE.

A very practical way of classifying trees according to size is the following: Young trees which have not yet reached a height of 3 feet are *seedlings* (fig. 19). They are called seedlings in spite of the fact that any tree, of whatever age, if it grew from a seed, is properly called a seedling tree. Trees from 3 to 10 feet in height are *small saplings*, and from 10 feet in height until they reach a diameter of 4 inches they are *large saplings*. *Small poles* are from 4 to 8 inches in diameter, and *large poles* from 8 to 12 inches in diameter. Trees from 1 to 2 feet through are *standards*, and, finally, all trees over 2 feet in diameter are *veterans*.

It is very important to remember that all these diameters are measured at the height of a man's chest, about 4 feet 6 inches from the ground. In forestry this is, roughly speaking, the general custom.

HOW THE CROP BEGINS.

Let us imagine an abundant crop of tree seeds lying on the ground in the forest. How they came there does not interest us at present; we do not care to know whether they were carried by the wind, as often happens with the winged seeds of many trees, such as pines and maples, whether the squirrels and birds dropped and planted some of them, as they frequently do acorns and chestnuts, or whether the old trees stood closely about and sowed the seeds themselves. We will suppose them to be all of one kind, and to be scattered in a place where the soil, the moisture, and the light are all just as they should be for their successful germination, and afterwards for the later stages of their lives. Even under the best conditions a considerable part of the fallen seed may never germinate, but in this case we will assume that half of it succeeds.

As each seed of our forest germinates and pushes its first slender rootlet downward into the earth, it has a very uncertain hold on life. Even for some time afterwards the danger from frost, dryness, and excessive moisture is very serious indeed, and there are many other foes by which the young seedlings may be overcome. It sometimes happens that great numbers of them perish in their earliest youth because their roots can not reach the soil through the thick, dry coating of dead leaves which covers it. But our young trees pass through the beginning of these dangers with comparatively little loss, and a plentiful crop of seedlings occupies the ground. As yet, however, each little tree stands free from those about it. As yet, too, the life of the young forest may be threatened or even destroyed by any one of the enemies already mentioned, or it may suffer just as severely if the cover of the older trees above it is too dense. In the beginning of their lives seedlings often require to be protected by the shade of their elders, but if this protection is too long continued they suffer for want of light, and are either killed outright or live only to drag on stunted and unhealthy lives.

THE FOREST COVER ESTABLISHED.

The crop which we are following has had a suitable proportion of shade and light during its earliest years, and the seedlings have spread until their crowns begin to meet. Hitherto each little tree has had all the space in the air and soil that it needed for the expansion of its top

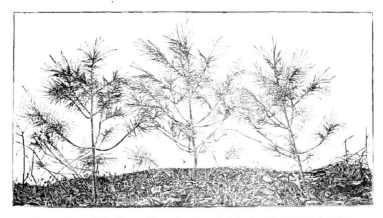

Fig. 20.—Young White Pine seedlings whose lower branches have just begun to interfere.

and roots. This would have been entirely good, except that meanwhile the soil about the trees has been more or less exposed to the sun and wind, and so has become dryer and less fertile than if it had been under cover, and consequently the growth has been slow. But now that the crowns are meeting, the situation becomes wonderfully changed. The soil begins to improve rapidly, because it is protected by the cover of the meeting crowns (fig. 20) and enriched by the leaves and twigs which fall from them.

THE BEGINNING OF THE STRUGGLE.

In so far the conditions of life are better, and in consequence the growth, and more especially the height growth, begins to show a marked increase. On the other hand, all the new strength is in

173

immediate demand. With the added vigor which the trees are now helping each other to attain, comes the most urgent need for rapid development for the decisive struggle at hand. The roots of the young trees contend with each other in the soil for moisture and the plant food which it contains, while in the air the crowns struggle for space and light. The latter is by far the more important battle. The victors in it overcome by greater rapidity of growth at the ends of the branches, for it is by growth there, and there only, that trees increase in height and spread of crown. Growth in this way was going on unchecked among the young trees before the crowns met, but now only the upward-growing branches can develop freely. The leaves at the ends of the side branches have now less room and, above all, less light, for they are crowded and thrust aside by those of the other trees. Very often they are bruised by thrashing against their neighbors when the wind blows, or even broken off while still in the bud. Leaves exposed to such dangers are unhealthy. They transpire less than the healthy undisturbed leaves of the upper part of the crown, and more and more of the undigested food from the roots goes to the stronger leaves at the top as the assimilating power of the side leaves dwindles with the loss of light. The young branches share the fortunes of their leaves and are vigorous or sickly according to the condition of the latter. For this reason the growth of the tops increases, while that of the lower lateral branches, as the tops cover them with a deeper and deeper shade, become less and less. Gradually it ceases altogether, and the branches perish. This process is called natural pruning, and from the time when it begins the existence of the young forest, unless it should be overtaken by fire or some other great calamity, is practically secure.

GROWTH IN HEIGHT.

At this time, as we have seen, the crowns of all the young trees are growing faster at the tops than at the sides, for there is unlimited room above. But some are growing faster than others, either because their roots are more developed or in better soil than those of the trees about them, because they have been freer from the attacks of insects and other enemies, or for some similar reasons. Some trees have an inborn tendency to grow faster than others of the same species in the same surroundings, just as one son in a family is often taller than the brothers with whom he was brought up.

Rapid growth in height, from whatever cause it proceeds, brings not only additional light and air to the tree which excels in it, but also the chance to spread laterally, and so to complete the defeat of its slower rivals by overtopping them.

17³

THE STRUGGLE CONTINUED.

Those trees which have gained this advantage over their neighbors are called dominant trees, while the surviving laggards in the race are said to be overtopped when they are hopelessly behind, and retarded when less badly beaten. Enormous numbers of seedlings and small saplings are suppressed and killed during the early youth of the forest. In the young crop which we are following many thousands perish upon every acre. Even the dominant trees, which are temporarily free when they rise above their neighbors, speedily come into conflict with each other as they spread, and in the end the greater portion is overcome. It is a very deadly struggle, but year by year the differences between the trees become less marked. Each separate individual clings to life with greater tenacity, the strife is more protracted and severe, and the number of trees which perish grows rapidly smaller. But so great is the pressure when dense groups of young trees are evenly matched in size and rate of growth that it is not very unusual to find the progress of the young forest in its early stages almost stopped and the trees uniformly sickly and undersized, on account of the crowding.

The forest we have been following has now passed through the small-sapling stage, and is composed chiefly, but not exclusively, of large saplings. Among the overtopped and retarded trees, which often remain in size classes which the dominant trees have long since outgrown, there are still many low saplings. Even between the dominant trees, in a healthy forest, there are always great differences. Increase in height is now going on rapidly among these high saplings, and either in this stage or the next a point is reached when the topmost branches make their longest yearly growth, which is one way of saying that the trees make their most rapid height growth as large saplings or small poles. Later on, as we shall see, these upper branches lengthen much more slowly, until, in standards and veterans, the growth in height is small, and in very old trees finally ceases altogether.

NATURAL PRUNING.

While the trees are pushing up most rapidly, the side branches are most quickly overshaded, and the process of natural pruning goes on with the greatest vigor. Natural pruning is the reason why old trees in a dense forest have only a small crown high in the air, and why their tall, straight trunks are clear of branches to such a height above the ground. The trunks of trees grown in the open, where even the lower limbs have abundance of light, are branched either quite to the ground or to within a short distance of it (fig. 21). But in the forest not only are the lower side branches continually dying for want of light, but the tree rids itself of them after they are dead and so frees its trunk from them entirely. When a branch dies the annual layer of new wood is no longer deposited upon it. Consequently the dead

FIG. 21.—Imperfect natural pruning of a White Pine that stood too much alone in early youth. Milford, Pa.

branch, where it is inserted in the tree, makes a little hole in the first coat of living tissue formed over the live wood after its death. The edges of this hole make a sort of collar about the base of the dead branch, and as a new layer is added each year they press it more and more tightly. So strong does this compression of the living wood become that at last what remains of the dead tissue has so little strength that the branch is broken off by a storm or even falls of its own weight. Then in a short time, if all goes well, the hole closes, and after a while little or no exterior trace of it remains. Knots, such as those which are found in boards, are the marks left in the trunk by branches which have disappeared.

THE CULMINATION OF GROWTH.

While the young trees are making clean trunks so rapidly during the period of greatest yearly height growth they are also making their greatest annual gains in diameter, for these two forms of growth generally culminate about the same time. A little later, if there is any difference, the young forest's highest yearly rate of growth in volume is also reached. For a time these three kinds of growth keep on at the same rate as in the past, but afterwards all three begin to decrease. Growth in diameter, and in volume also, if the trees are sound, goes on until extreme old age, but height growth sinks very low while the two others are still strong. For many years before this happens the struggle between the trees has not been so deadly, because they have been almost without the means of overtopping one another. When the end of the period of principal height growth is reached the trees are interfering with each other very little, and the struggle for life begins again in a different way. As the principal height growth ceases, and the tops no longer shoot up rapidly above the side branches, the crowns lose their pointed shape and become comparatively flat. The chief reason why trees stop growing in height is that they are not able to keep the upper parts of their crowns properly supplied with water above a certain distance from the ground. This distance varies in different kinds of trees, and with the health and vigor of the tree in each species, but there is a limit in every case above which the water does not reach. The power of the pumping machinery, more than any other quality, determines the height of the tree.

THE END OF THE STRUGGLE.

Now that the tree can no longer expand at the top, it must either suffer a great loss in the number of its leaves or be able to spread at the sides; for it is clear that not nearly so many leaves can be exposed to the light in the flattened crown as in the pointed one, just as a pointed roof has more surface than a flat one (fig. 22). It is just at this time, too, that the trees begin to bear seed most abundantly, and it is of the greatest importance to each tree that its digestive apparatus in the leaves should be able to furnish a large supply of digested food. Consequently the struggle for space is fiercely renewed, only now the trees no longer attempt to overtop one another, having lost the power, but to crowd one another away at the sides. The whole forest might suffer severely at this point from a deadlock such as sometimes happens in early youth were it not for the fact that the trees, as they grow older, become more and more sensitive to any shade. Many species which stand crowding fairly well in youth can not thrive in age unless their crowns are completely free on every side. Each of the victors in this last phase of the struggle is the survivor of hundreds (or sometimes even of thousands) of seedlings. Among very numerous competitors they have shown themselves to be the best adapted to their surroundings.

Natural selection has made it clear that these are the best trees for the place. These are also the trees which bear the seed whence the

 younger generations spring. Their offspring will inherit their fitness to a greater or less degree, and in their turn will be subjected to the same rigorous test, by which only the best are allowed to reach maturity. Under this sifting out of the weak and the unfit, our native trees have been prepared through thousands of generations to meet the conditions under which they must live. This is why they are so much more apt to succeed than species from abroad, which have not been fitted for our climate and soil by natural selection.

The forest which we saw first in the seed has now passed through all the more vigorous and active stages of its life. The trees have become standards and veterans, and large enough to be valuable for lumber. Rapid growth in height has long been at an end, diameter growth is slow, and the forest as a whole is increasing very little in volume as time goes on. The trees are ripe for the harvest.

Out of the many things which might happen to our mature forest, we will only consider three.

DEATH FROM WEAKNESS AND DECAY.

In the first place, we will suppose that it stands untouched until, like the trees of the virgin forest, it meets its death from weakness and decay.

The trees of the mature primeval forest live on, if no accidents intervene, almost at peace among themselves. At length all conflict between them ends. The whole power of each tree is strained in a new struggle against death, until at last it fails. One by one the old trees disappear. But long before they go the forerunners of a new generation have sprung up wherever light came in between their isolated crowns. As the old trees fall, with intervals often of many years between their deaths, young growth of various ages rises to take their place (fig. 23), and when the last of the old forest crop has vanished there may be differences of a hundred years among the young trees which succeed it. An even-aged crop of considerable extent, such as we have been considering, is not usual in the virgin forest, where trees of very different ages grow side by side, and when it does occur the next generation is far less uniform. The forest whose history has just been sketched was chosen, not because it represents the most

Fig. 23.—Young growth under old trees. Southwestern Oregon.

common type of natural forest, but because it illustrates better than any other the progress of forest growth.

The wood of a tree which dies in the forest is almost wholly wasted. For a time the rotting trunk may serve to retain moisture, but there is little use for the carbon, oxygen, and hydrogen which make up its greater part. The mineral constituents alone form a useful fertilizer, but most often there is already an abundance of similar material in the soil. Not only is the old tree lost, but ever since its maturity it has done little more than intercept, to no good purpose, the light which would otherwise have given vitality to a valuable crop of younger trees. It is only when the ripe wood is harvested properly and in time that the forest attains its highest usefulness.

DESTRUCTIVE LUMBERING.

A second thing which may happen to a forest is to be cut down without care for the future (fig. 24). The yield of a forest lumbered in the usual way is more or less thoroughly harvested, it is true, but at an enormous cost to the forest. Ordinary lumbering injures or destroys the young growth, both in the present and for the future, provokes and feeds fires, and does harm of many other kinds. In many cases

FIG. 24.—Destructive lumbering in the Coast Redwood belt, Humboldt County, Cal.

its result is to annihilate the productive capacity of forest land for tens or scores of years to come.

CONSERVATIVE LUMBERING.

Correct methods of forestry, on the other hand, maintain and increase both the productiveness and the capital value of forest land; harvest the yield far more completely than ordinary lumbering, although less rapidly; prepare for, encourage, and preserve the young growth; tend to keep out fires; and in general draw from the forest, while protecting it, the best return which it is capable of giving.

The application of such methods is the third possibility for the crop just described, and in their application is to be found the wisest, safest, and most satisfactory way of dealing with the forest.

There are still many places in the United States, however, where transportation is so costly that, as yet, forestry will not pay from a business point of view.

ENEMIES OF THE FOREST.

The forest is threatened by many enemies, of which fire and reckless lumbering are the worst. In the United States sheep grazing and wind come next. Cattle and horses do much less damage than sheep, and snow break is less costly than windfall. Landslides, floods, insects, and fungi are sometimes very harmful. In certain situations numbers of trees are killed by lightning, which has also been known to set the woods on fire, and the forest is attacked in many other ways. For example, birds and squirrels often prevent young growth by devouring great quantities of nuts and other seeds, while porcupines and mice frequently kill young trees by gnawing away their bark.

MAN AND NATURE IN THE FOREST.

Most of these foes may be called natural enemies, for they would injure the forest to a greater or less extent if the action of man were altogether removed. Wild animals would take the place of domestic sheep and cattle to some degree, and fire, wind, and insects would still attack the forest. But many the most serious dangers to the forest are of human origin. So the destructive lumbering (fig. 24) and excessive taxation on forest lands to which much bad lumbering is directly due. So heavy are these taxes, for in many cases they amount to 5 or even 6 per cent of the actual market value of the forests, that the owners can not afford to pay them and hold their lands. Consequently they are tempted to cut or sell their timber in haste and without regard to the future. When the timber is gone the owners refuse to pay taxes any longer, and the devastated lands revert to the State. Many thousands of square miles of forest have been ruined by reckless lumbering, because heavy taxes forced the owners to realize quickly and once for all upon their forest land, instead of cutting it in a way to insure valuable future crops. For the same reason many counties are now poor that might, with reasonable taxation of timber land, have been flourishing and rich.

GRAZING IN THE FOREST.

Whether grazing animals are comparatively harmless to the forest or among its most dangerous enemies depends on the age and character of the wood as well as upon the kind of animals that graze. A young forest is always more exposed to such injury than an old one, and steep slopes are more subject to damage than more level ground. Whether the young trees are conifers, and so more likely to suffer from trampling than from being eaten, or broadleaf trees, and so more likely to be devoured, they should be protected from pasturing animals until they are large enough to be out of danger.

GRAZING AND FIRE.

Grazing in the forest does harm in three ways. First, it is a fertile cause of forest fires. Burning the soil cover of grass and other plants improves the grazing, either permanently, by destroying the forest and so extending the area of pasturage, or temporarily, by

Fig. 25.—Band of sheep in a forest reserve. Cascade Mountains, Waco County, Oreg. Altitude, 5,800 feet.

improving the quality of the feed. For one or the other of these objects, but chiefly for the latter, vast areas are annually burned over in nearly every part of the United States where trees grow. The great majority of these fires do not kill the old trees, but the harm they do the forest and, eventually, the forage plants themselves, is very serious indeed. The sheepmen of the West are commonly accused of setting many forest fires to improve the grazing, and they are also vigorously defended from this charge. But the fact remains that large areas where sheep now graze would be covered with forests except for the action of more or less recent fires.

174

TRAMPLING.

Trampling is the second way in which grazing animals injure the forest. Cattle and horses do comparatively little harm, although their hoofs compact the soil and often tear loose the slender rootlets of small trees. Sheep, on the contrary, are exceedingly harmful (fig. 25), especially on steep slopes and where the soil is loose. In such places their small, sharp hoofs cut and powder the soil, break and overthrow the young trees, and often destroy promising young forests altogether. In many places the effect of the trampling is to destroy the forest floor and to interfere very seriously with the flow of streams. In the Alps of southern France sheep grazing led to the destruction, first, of the mountain forests, and then of the grass which had replaced them, and thus left the soil fully exposed to the rain. Great floods followed, beds of barren stones were spread over the fertile fields by the force of the water, and many rich valleys were almost or altogether depopulated. Besides the loss occasioned in this way, it has cost the French people tens of millions of dollars to repair the damage begun by the sheep, and the task is not yet finished. The loss to the nation is enormously greater than any gain from the mountain pastures could have been, and even the sheep owners themselves, for whose profit the damage was done, were losers in the end, for their industry in that region was utterly destroyed.

BROWSING.

The third way in which grazing animals injure the forest is by feeding on the young trees. In the western part of the United States, where most of the forests are evergreen, this is far less important than the damage from either fire or trampling, for sheep and other animals seldom eat young conifers if they can get other food. Even where broadleaf trees prevail browsing rarely leads to the destruction of any forest, although it commonly results in scanty young growth, often maimed and unsound as well. Goats are especially harmful, and where they abound the healthy reproduction of broadleaf trees is practically impossible. In the United States they are fortunately not common. Cattle devour tender young shoots and branches in vast quantities, often living for months on little else, and sheep are destructive in the same way. Hogs also find a living in the forest, but they are less harmful, because a large part of their food consists of seeds and nuts. East of the Great Plains very large numbers of cattle and hogs are turned into the woods, but sheep grazing in the forest is most widely developed in the West, and especially in California, where it should be prevented altogether, in Oregon and Washington, where it should be regulated and restricted, and in some interior regions, like Wyoming and New Mexico, where it should be rigidly excluded from all steep mountain regions, and carefully regulated on more level ground.

FOREST INSECTS.

Insects are constantly injuring the forest, just as year by year they bring loss to the farm. Occasionally their ravages attain enormous proportions. Thus a worm, which afterwards develops into a sawfly, has since 1882 killed nearly every full-grown larch in the Adirondacks by eating away the leaves. Even the small and vigorous larches do not escape altogether from these attacks. Conifers, such as the larch and spruce, are much more likely to suffer from the attacks of insects than broadleaf trees. About the year 1876 small bark beetles began to kill the mature spruce trees in the Adirondacks, and ten years later, when the worst of the attack was past, the forest had been practically deprived of all its largest spruces. This pest is still at work in northern New Hampshire and in Maine.

FOREST FUNGI.

Fungi attack the forest in many ways. Some kill the roots of trees, some grow upward from the ground into the trees and change the sound wood of the trunks to a useless rotten mass, and the minute spores (or seeds) of others float through the air and come in contact with every external part of the tree above ground. Wherever the wood is exposed there is danger that spores will find lodgment and breed disease. This is a strong reason why all wounds, such as those made in pruning, should be covered with some substance like paint or tar to exclude the air and the spores it carries.

WIND IN THE FOREST.

The effect of wind in the virgin forest is not wholly injurious. Although in many regions it overthrows great numbers of old trees, their removal is usually followed by a vigorous young growth where the old trees stood. In this way the wind helps to keep the forest full of young and healthy trees. But it also breaks and blows down great numbers of useful growing members of the forest (fig. 26). Much of this windfall occurs among shallow-rooted trees, or where the ground is soft because soaked with water, or where the trees have been weakened by unsoundness or fire. Some storms are strong enough to break the trees they can not overthrow. Damage from wind is not uncommon in many parts of the United States, and in places the loss from it is very serious. Near the town of High Springs, in Alachua County, Fla., for example, in a region very subject to storms there is a tract of many square miles, once covered with

Longleaf Pine, over which practically all the trees were killed by a great storm several years ago. Some were thrown flat, some were so racked and so broken in the top that they died, and very many were

Fig. 25.—A windfall in the Olympic Forest Reserve, Washington.

snapped off 15 to 30 feet above the ground. There is little use in taking precautions against such great calamities, yet the loss from windfall may be very much reduced by judicious cutting. An unbroken forest is least exposed.

173

SNOW IN THE FOREST.

Snow often loads down, breaks, and crushes tall young trees (fig. 27), especially if wet snow falls heavily before the broadleaf trees have shed their foliage in the fall. Such injury is difficult to guard against,

Fig. 27.—A young spruce loaded with snow. Avalanche Lake, Adirondack Mountains, New York.

but it is well to know that very slim, tall trees suffer more than those whose growth in diameter and height have kept better pace with each other. In many regions snow is so useful in protecting the soil and the young trees that the harm it does is quite overbalanced by its benefits.

FOREST FIRES.

Of all the foes which attack the woodlands of North America no other is so terrible as fire. Forest fires spring from many different causes. They are often kindled along railroads by sparks from the locomotives. Carelessness is responsible for many fires. Settlers and farmers clearing land or burning grass and brush often allow the fire to escape into the woods. Someone may drop a half-burned match or the glowing tobacco of a pipe or cigar, or a hunter or prospector may neglect to extinguish his camp fire, or may build it where it will burrow into the thick duff far beyond his reach, to smolder for days, or

Fig. 28.—The rotting stubs of fire-killed veterans of Red Fir surrounded by young standards of Red Fir and Western Hemlock. Olympic Forest Reserve, Washington.

weeks, and perhaps to break out as a destructive fire long after he is gone. Many fires are set for malice or revenge, and the forest is often burned over by huckleberry pickers to increase the next season's growth of berries, or by the owners of cattle or sheep to make better pasture for their herds.

Fire sometimes renews an old forest by killing the veterans and so permitting vigorous young trees to take their place (fig. 28).

There is danger from forest fires in the dry portions of the spring and summer, but those which do most harm usually occur in the fall. At whatever time of the year they appear, their destructive power depends very much on the wind. They can not travel against it except when burning up hill, and not even then if the wind is strong. The wind may give them strength and speed by driving them swiftly through unburned, inflammable forests, or it may extinguish the fiercest fire in a short time by turning it back over its path, where there is nothing left to burn. In fighting forest fires the wind is always the first thing to consider, and its direction must be carefully watched. A sudden change of wind may check a fire, or may turn it off in a new direction and perhaps threaten the lives of the men at work by driving it suddenly down upon them.

HISTORIC FOREST FIRES.

When all the conditions are favorable, forest fires sometimes reach gigantic proportions. A few such fires have attained historic importance. One of these is the Miramichi fire of 1825. It began its greatest destruction about 1 o'clock in the afternoon of October 7 at a place about 60 miles above the town of Newcastle, on the Miramichi River in New Brunswick. Before 10 o'clock at night it was 20 miles below Newcastle. In nine hours it had destroyed a belt of forest 80 miles long and 25 miles wide. Over more than two and a half million acres almost every living thing was killed. Even the fish were afterwards found dead in heaps along the river banks. Five hundred and ninety buildings were burned, and a number of towns, including Newcastle, Chatham, and Douglastown, were destroyed. One hundred and sixty persons perished and nearly a thousand head of stock. The loss from the Miramichi fire is estimated at $300,000, not including the value of the timber.

In the majority of such forest fires as this the destruction of the timber is a more serious loss by far than that of the cattle and buildings, for it carries with it the impoverishment of a whole region for tens or even hundreds of years afterwards. The loss of the stumpage value of the timber at the time of the fire is but a small part of the damage to the neighborhood. The wages that would have been earned in lumbering, added to the value of the produce that would have been purchased to supply the lumber camps, and the taxes that would have been devoted to roads and other public improvements, furnish a much truer measure of how much, sooner or later, it costs a region when its forests are destroyed by fire.

The Peshtigo fire of October, 1871, was still more severe than the Miramichi. It covered an area of over 2,000 square miles in Wisconsin, and involved a loss, in timber and other property, of many millions of dollars. Between 1,200 and 1,500 persons perished, including nearly half the population of Peshtigo, at that time a town of 2,000 inhabitants. Other fires of about the same time were most destructive in Michigan. A strip about 40 miles wide and 180 miles long, extending across the central part of the State from Lake Michigan to Lake Huron,

43

was devastated. The estimated loss in timber was about 4,000,000,000 feet board measure and in money over $10,000,000. Several hundred persons perished.

In the early part of September, 1881, great fires covered more than 1,800 square miles in various parts of Michigan. The estimated loss in property, in addition to many hundred thousand acres of valuable timber, was more than $2,300,000. Over 5,000 persons were made destitute, and the number of lives lost is variously estimated at from 150 to 500.

The most destructive fire of more recent years was that which started near Hinckley, Minn., September 1, 1894. While the area burned over was less than in some other great fires, the loss of life and property was very heavy. Hinckley and six other towns were destroyed, about 500 lives were lost, more than 2,000 persons were left destitute, and the estimated loss in property of various kinds was $25,000,000. Except for the heroic conduct of locomotive engineers and other railroad men the loss of life would have been far greater.

This fire was all the more deplorable because it was wholly unnecessary. For many days before the high wind came and drove it into uncontrollable fury it was burning slowly close to the town of Hinckley and could have been put out.

MEANS OF DEFENSE.

The means of fighting forest fires are not everywhere the same, for they burn in many different ways; but in every case the best time to fight a fire is at the beginning, before it has had time to spread. A delay of even a very few minutes may permit a fire that at first could easily have been extinguished to gather headway and get altogether beyond control.

When there is but a thin covering of leaves and other waste on the ground a fire usually can not burn very hotly or move with much speed. The fires in most hardwood forests are of this kind. They seldom kill large trees, but they destroy seedlings and saplings and kill the bark and older trees in places near the ground. The hollows at the foot of old chestnuts and other large trees are often the result of these fires which occur again and again, and so enlarge the wounds instead of allowing them to heal. Moderate fires also occur in dense coniferous forests when only the top of a thick layer of duff is dry enough to burn. The heat may not be great enough to kill any but the smallest and tenderest younger trees, but that does not mean that such fires do no harm. The life of the forest depends on just such young growth, and when the forest floor, which is so necessary both to the trees and for the water supply, is injured or destroyed by fire, the forest suffers harm.

SURFACE FIRES.

Surface fires (fig. 29) may be checked if they are feeble by beating them out with green branches or by raking the leaves away from a narrow strip across their course. The best tool for this purpose is a four-tined pitchfork or a common stable fork. In sandy regions a thin and narrow belt of sand is easily and quickly sprinkled over the ground with a shovel, and will check the spread of a weak fire, or even of a comparatively hot one if there is no wind. Dirt or sand thrown on a burning fire is one of the best of all means for putting it out.

FIG. 29.—A surface fire burning slowly against the wind, southern New Jersey.

In dense forests with a heavy forest floor fires are often hot enough not only to kill the standing timber but to consume the trunks and branches altogether, and even to follow the roots far down into the ground. In forests of this kind fire spreads easily, creeping along on the surface or through the duff or under the bark of rotting fallen trees. In the same way it climbs dead standing trees and breaks out in bursts of flame high in the air. Dead trees help powerfully to spread a fire, for in high winds loose pieces of their burning bark are carried to almost incredible distances and drop into the dry forest far ahead, while in calm weather they scatter burning fragments all about them when they fall. (See fig. 30.)

GROUND FIRES.

When the duff is very deep or the soil peaty a fire may burn beneath
the surface of the ground for weeks or even months, sometimes showing its presence by a little smoke, sometimes without giving any sign
of life. Even a heavy rain may fail to quench a fire of this kind,
which often breaks out again long after it is believed to be entirely
extinct. Fires which thus burn into the ground can sometimes be

FIG. 30.—The effect of repeated fires. Not only the old trees are dead, but the seedlings which
succeeded them have perished also. Western Yellow Pine in the Black Hills Forest Reserve, South
Dakota.

checked only by digging a trench through the layer of decaying wood
and other vegetable matter to the mineral soil beneath. Ground fires
usually burn much more slowly than surface fires, but they are excep-
tionally long lived and very hard to put out. It is of the first importance to attack such fires quickly before they have had time to burrow
far beneath the surface of the ground. Surface fires are usually far

less troublesome, but in either case fires which kill the trees are generally repeated again and again until the dead timber is consumed (fig. 31).

Fig. 21.—The result of recurring fires. The forest floor has disappeared and the pure white sand is left without covering. Southern New Jersey.

BACK FIRING.

The most dangerous and destructive forest fires are those which run both along the ground and in the tops of the trees. When a fire becomes intensely hot on the ground, it may run up the bark, especially

Fig. 32.—Setting a back fire on the windward side of a road. Southern New Jersey.

if the trees are conifers, and burn in the crowns. Such fires are the fiercest and most destructive of all. Traveling sometimes faster than a man can run, they consume enormous quantities of valuable timber, burn fences, buildings, and domestic animals, and endanger or even destroy human lives. They can be checked only by rain or change of wind, or by meeting some barrier which they can not pass. A barrier of this kind is often made by starting another fire some distance ahead of the principal one. This back fire, as it is called, must be allowed to burn only against the wind and toward the main fire, so that when the two fires meet both must go out for lack of fuel. To prevent it from moving with the wind, a back fire should always be started on the windward side of a road (fig. 32) or a raked or sanded strip, or some other line which it can be kept from crossing. If it is allowed to escape it may become as dangerous as the main fire itself. Back fires are sometimes driven beyond control by a change of wind, but the chief danger from their use is caused by

Fig.   A back line along a railroad with trees cut and used, separated by a double row of trees extended to catch the sparks.

persons who, in excitement or fright, light them at the wrong time or in the wrong place. Still, there is no other means of fighting fires so powerful and none so effective when rightly used.

FIRE LINES.

Fire lines—strips kept free from all inflammable material by burning or otherwise—are very useful in checking small fires and of great value as lines of defense in fighting large ones. They are also very effective in keeping fires out of the woods, as, for example, along railroad tracks (fig. 33). But without men to do the fighting they are of as little use against really dangerous fires as forts without soldiers against invading armies.

FARMERS' BULLETINS.

The following is a list of the Farmers' Bulletins available for distribution, showing the number, title, and size in pages of each. Copies will be sent to any address on application to any Senator, Representative, or Delegate in Congress, or to the Secretary of Agriculture, Washington, D. C. The missing numbers have been discontinued, being superseded by later bulletins.

CPSIA information can be obtained
at www.ICGtesting.com
Printed in the USA
LVHW101047021219
639151LV00009B/96/P